Presenting:

HELLO YELLOW

LET'S SAY HELLO TO SOME THINGS THAT ARE YELLOW!

WORDS & ART BY: BRIANNA DAVIS

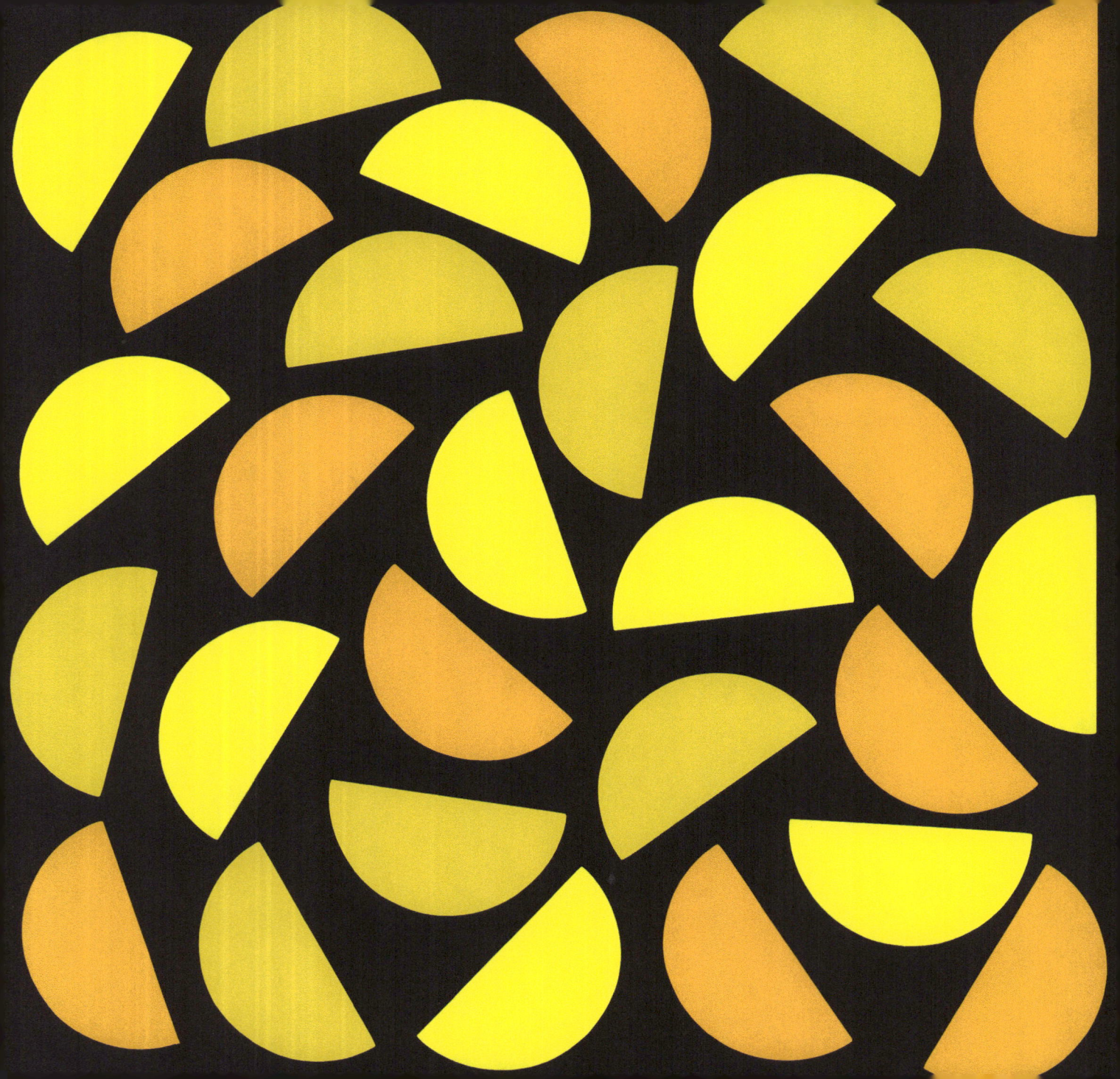

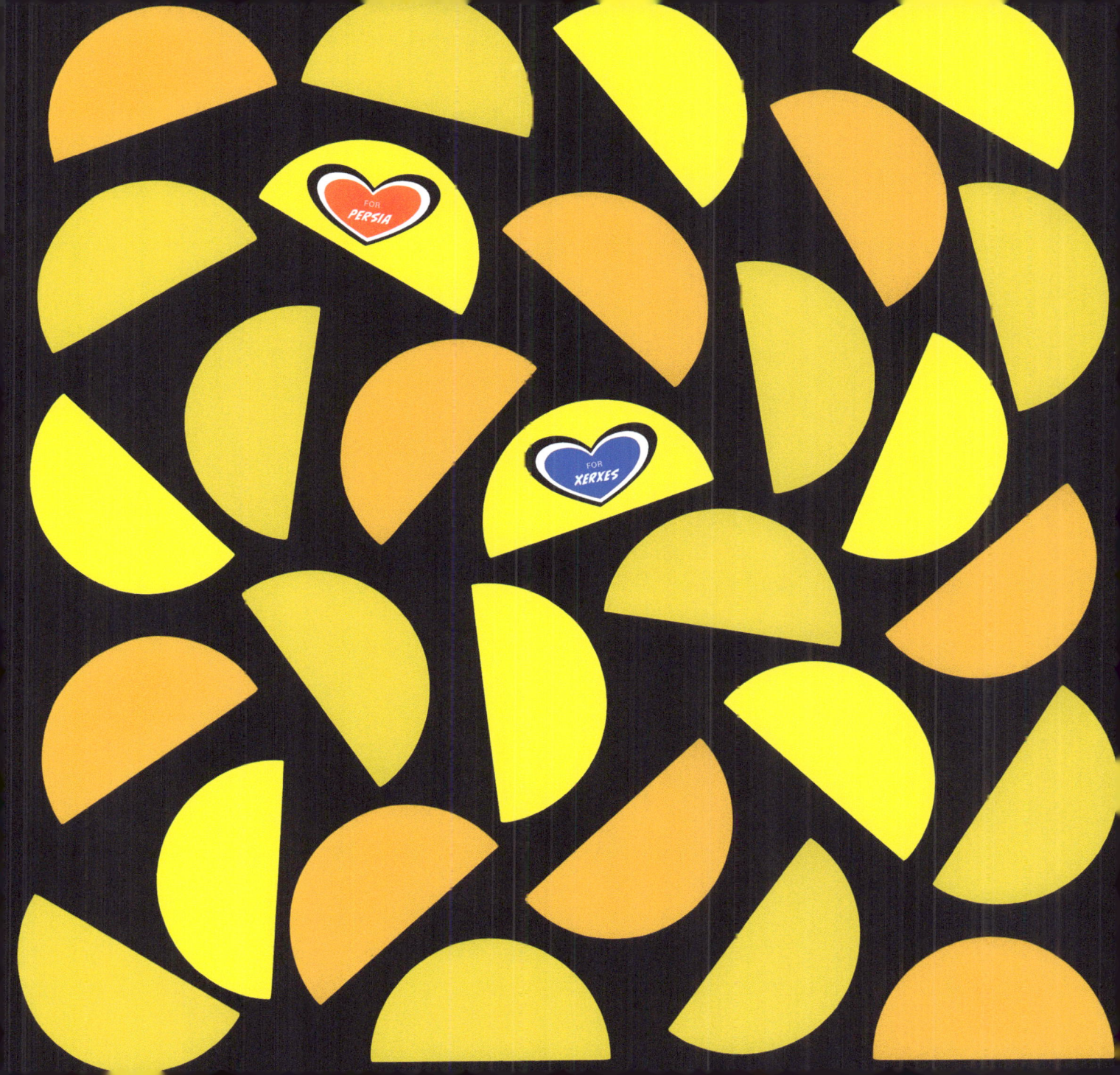

YELLOW

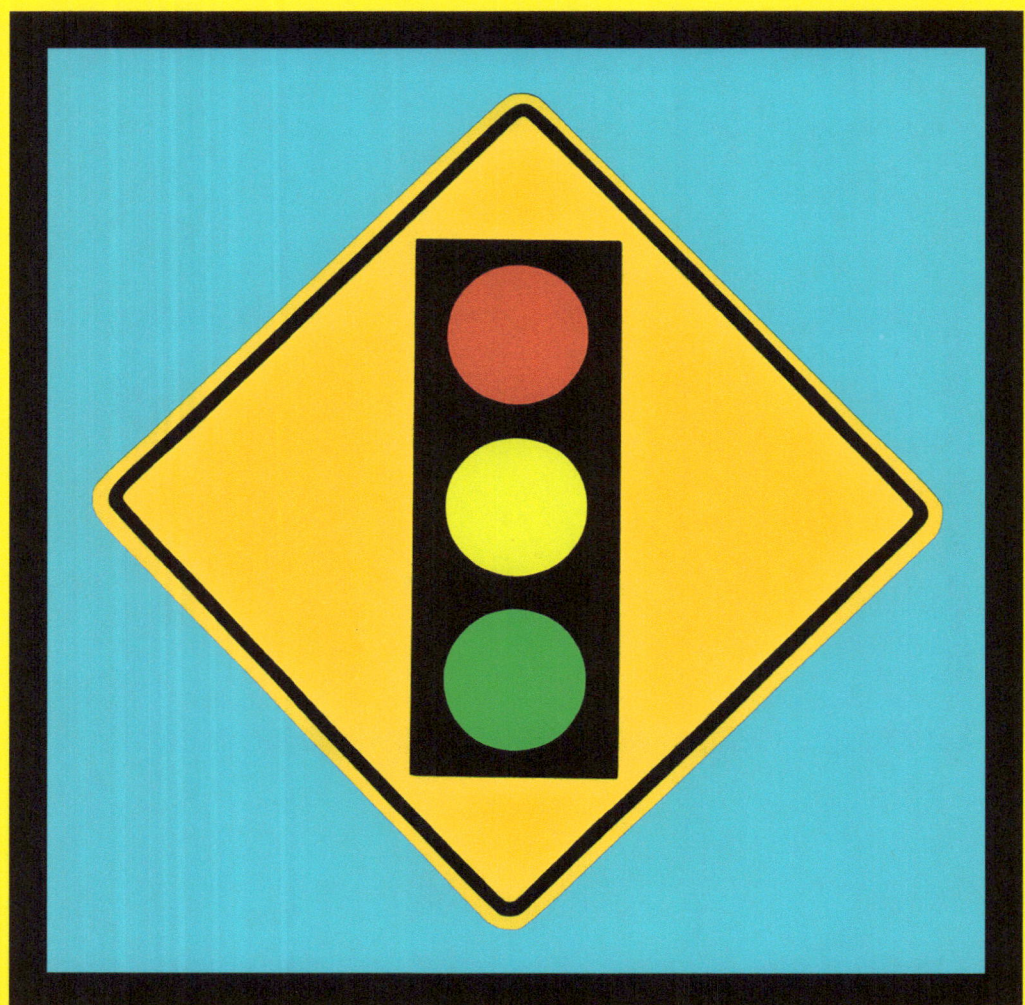

YELLOW IS EASY TO SPOT BECAUSE IT'S SO BRIGHT...

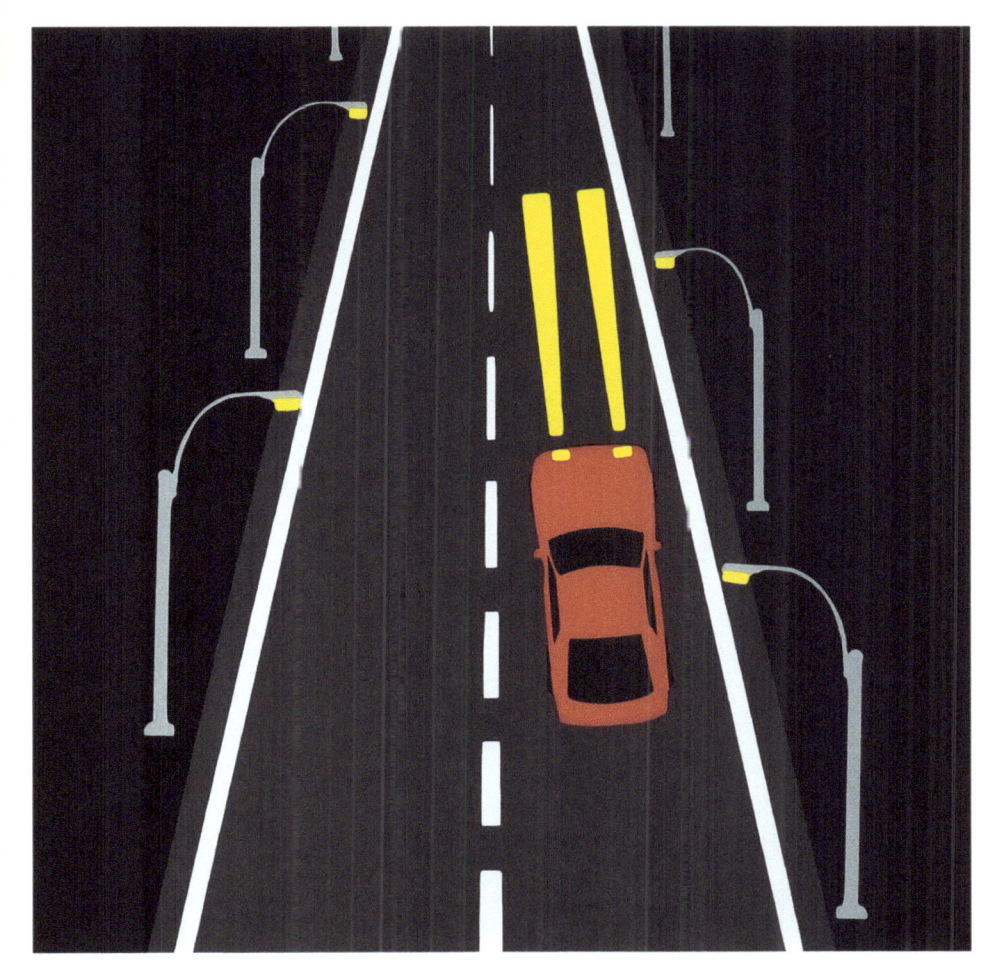

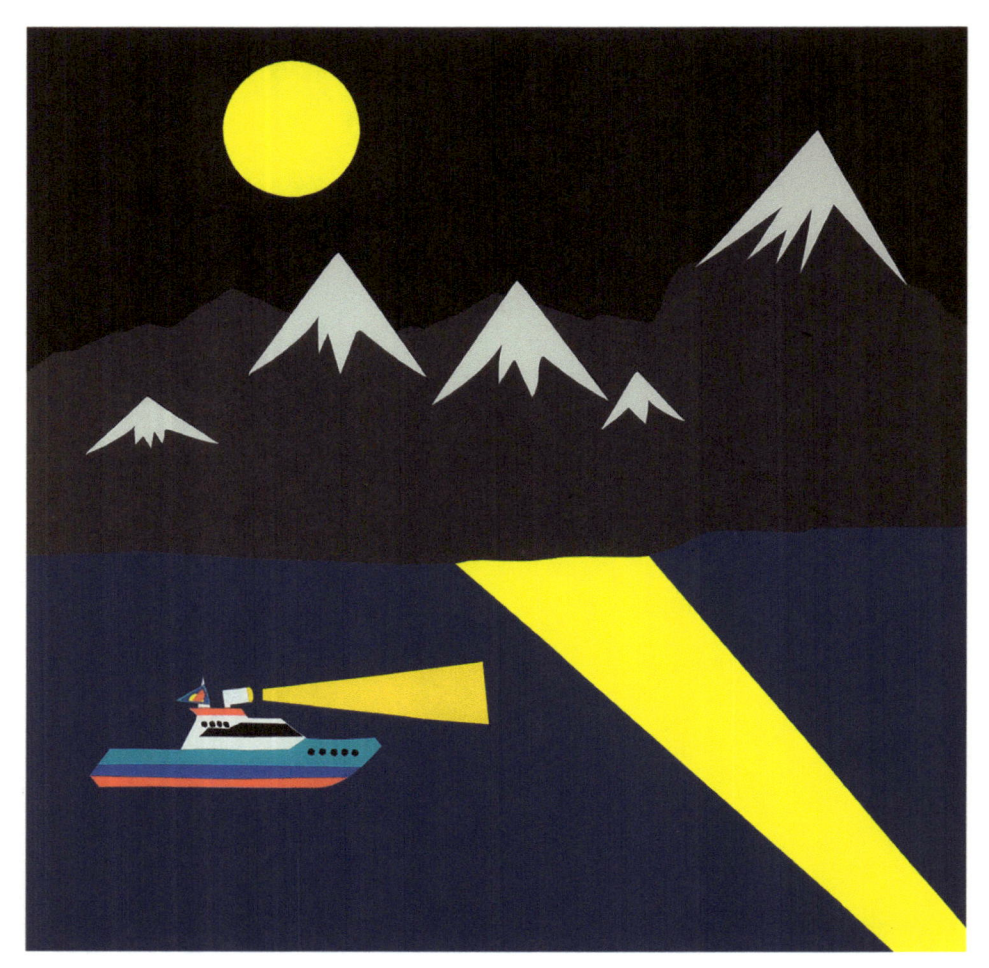

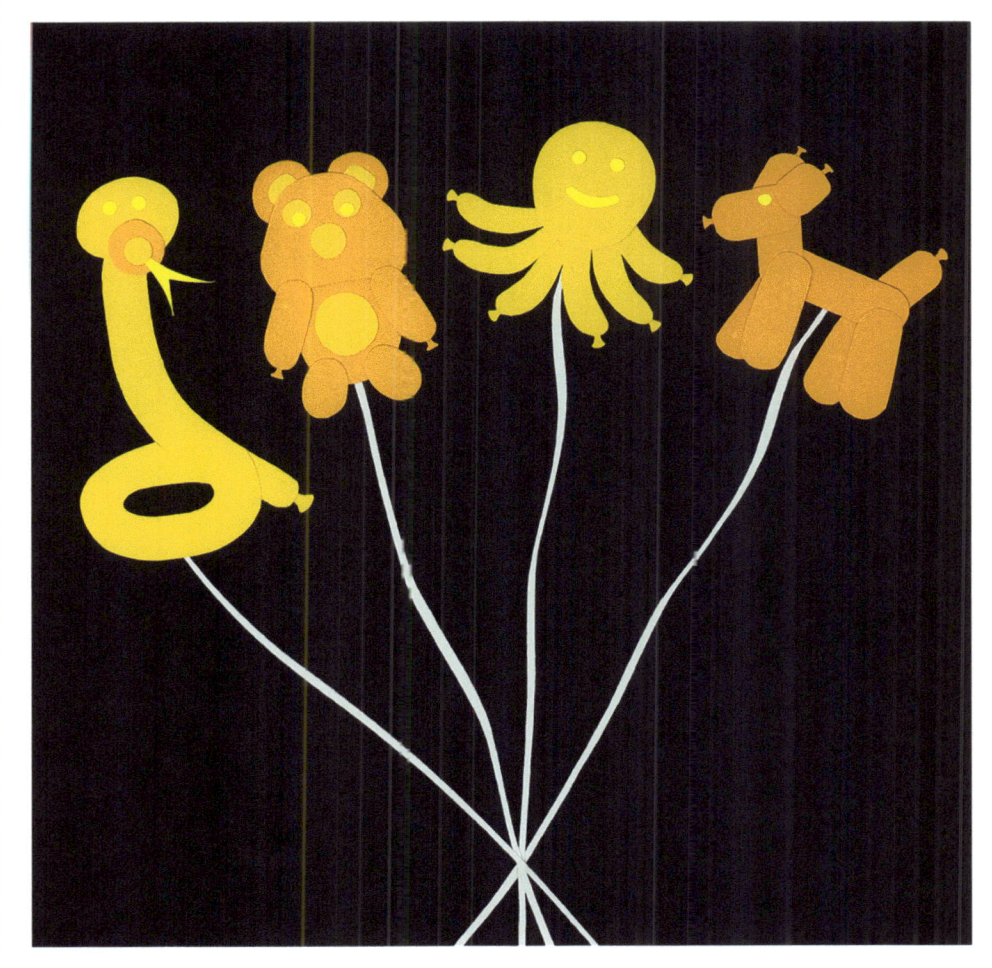

AND STARS IN THIS MEDLEY OF ANIMAL SHAPED BALLOONS!

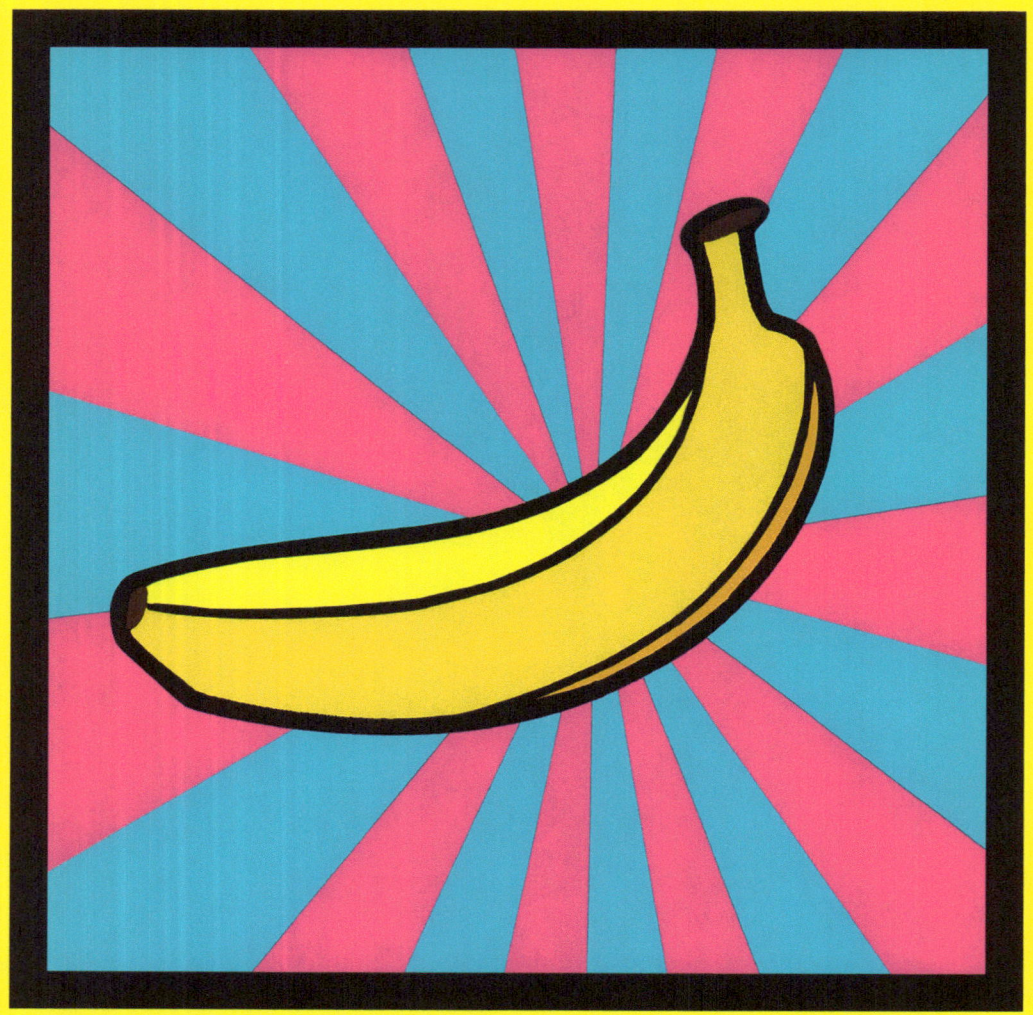

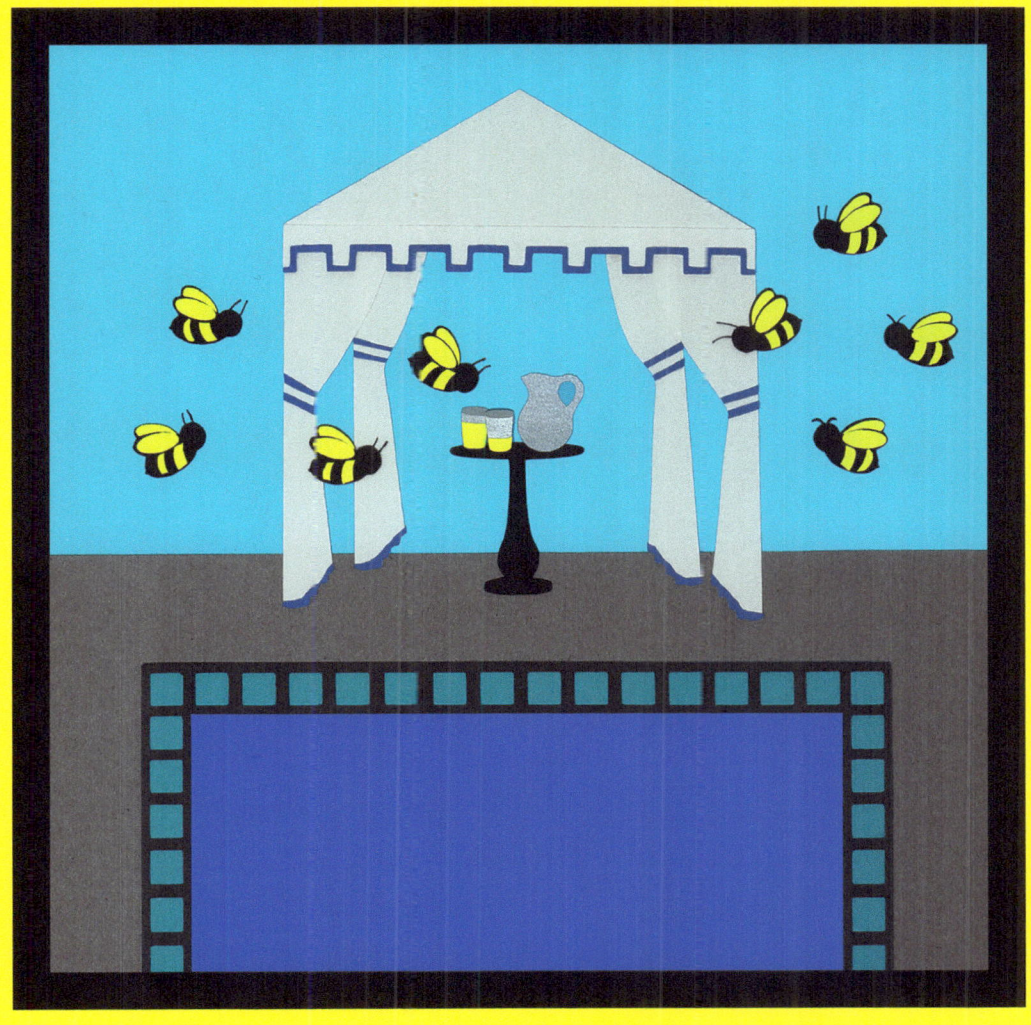

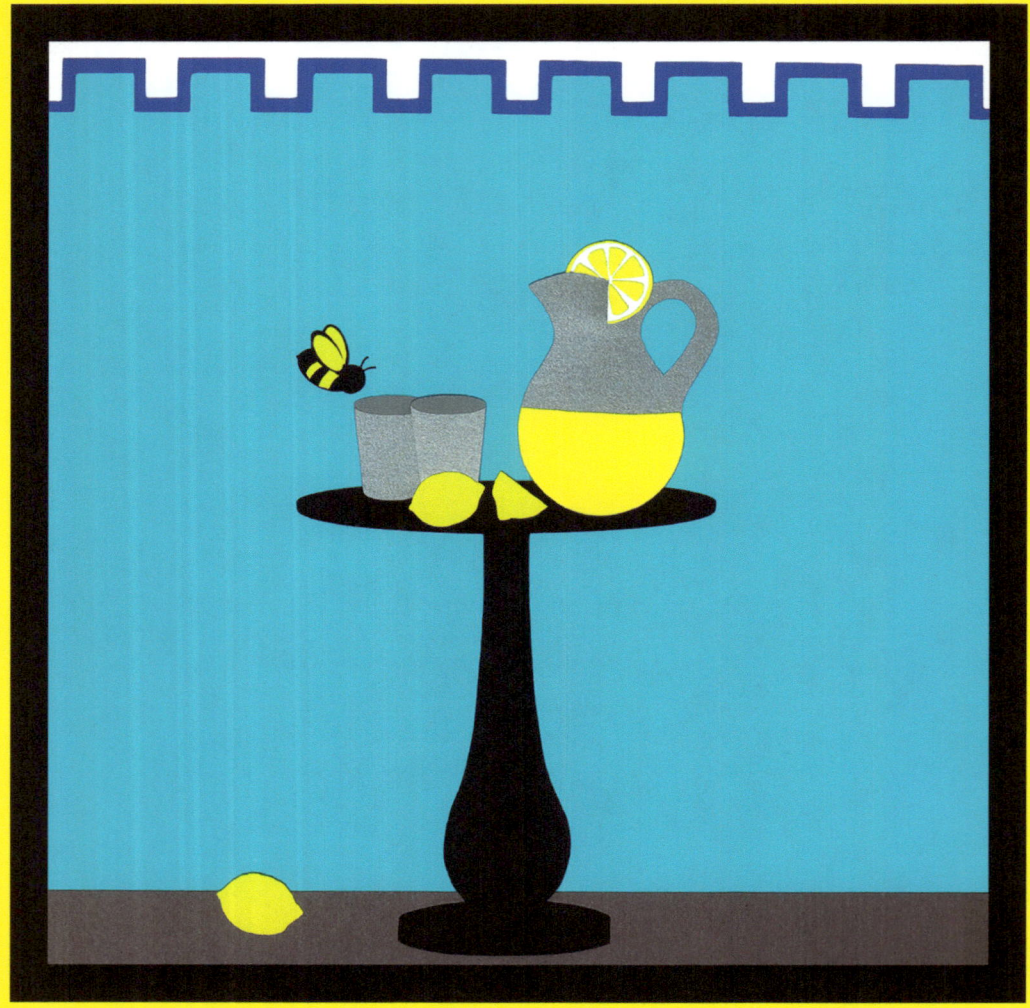

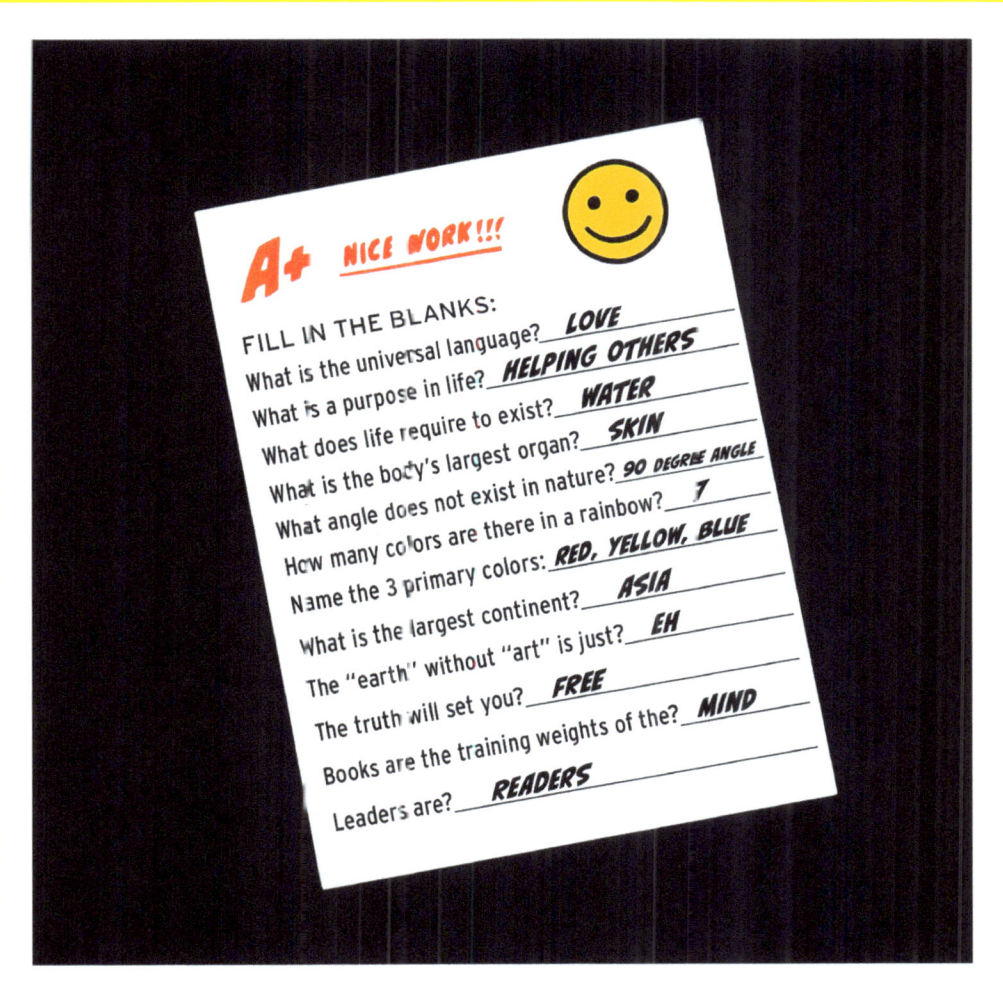

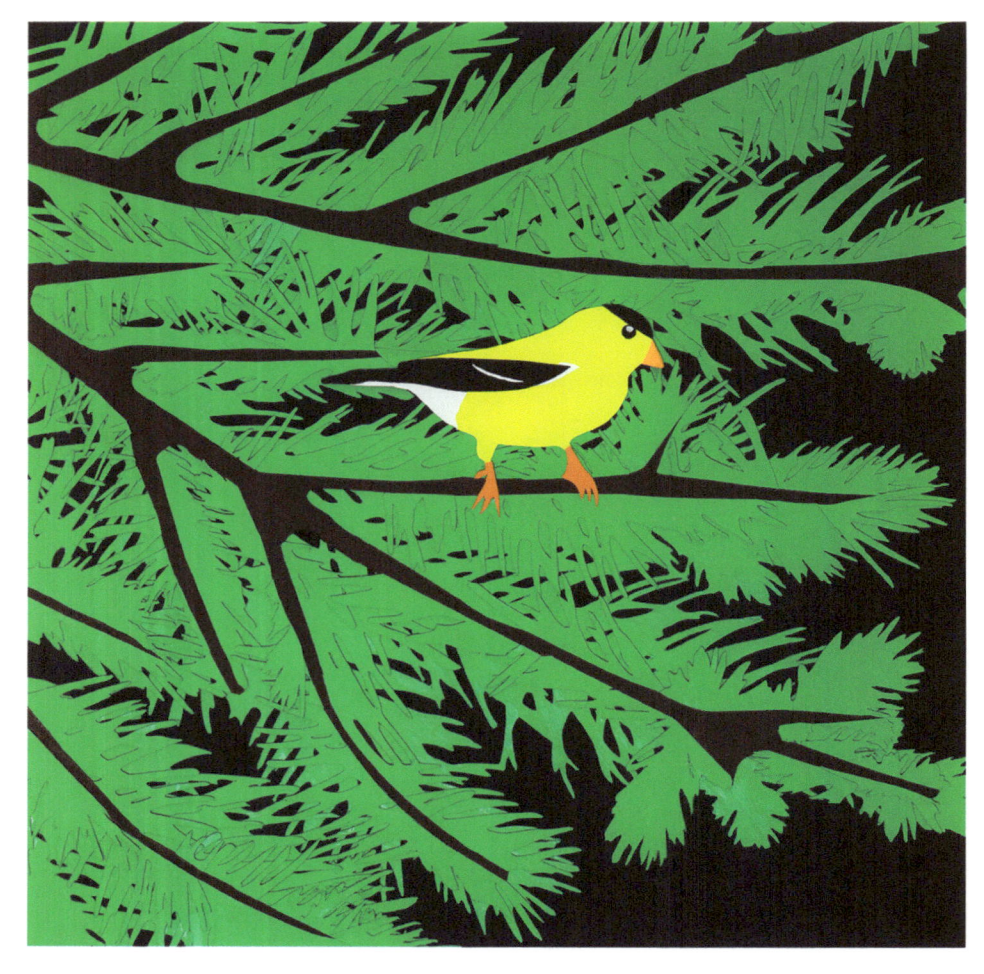

IF YOU GO BIRDWATCHING, A GOLDFINCH IS A SIGHT TO SEE...

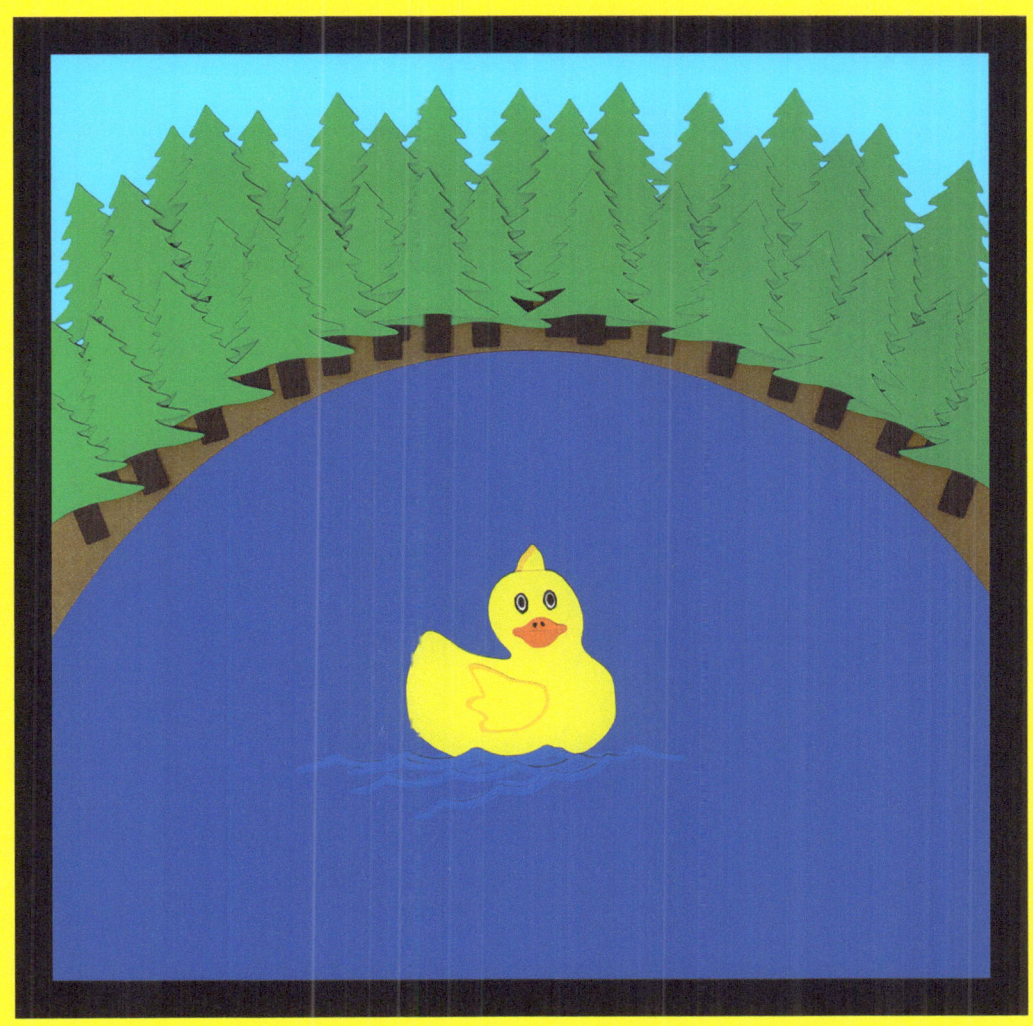

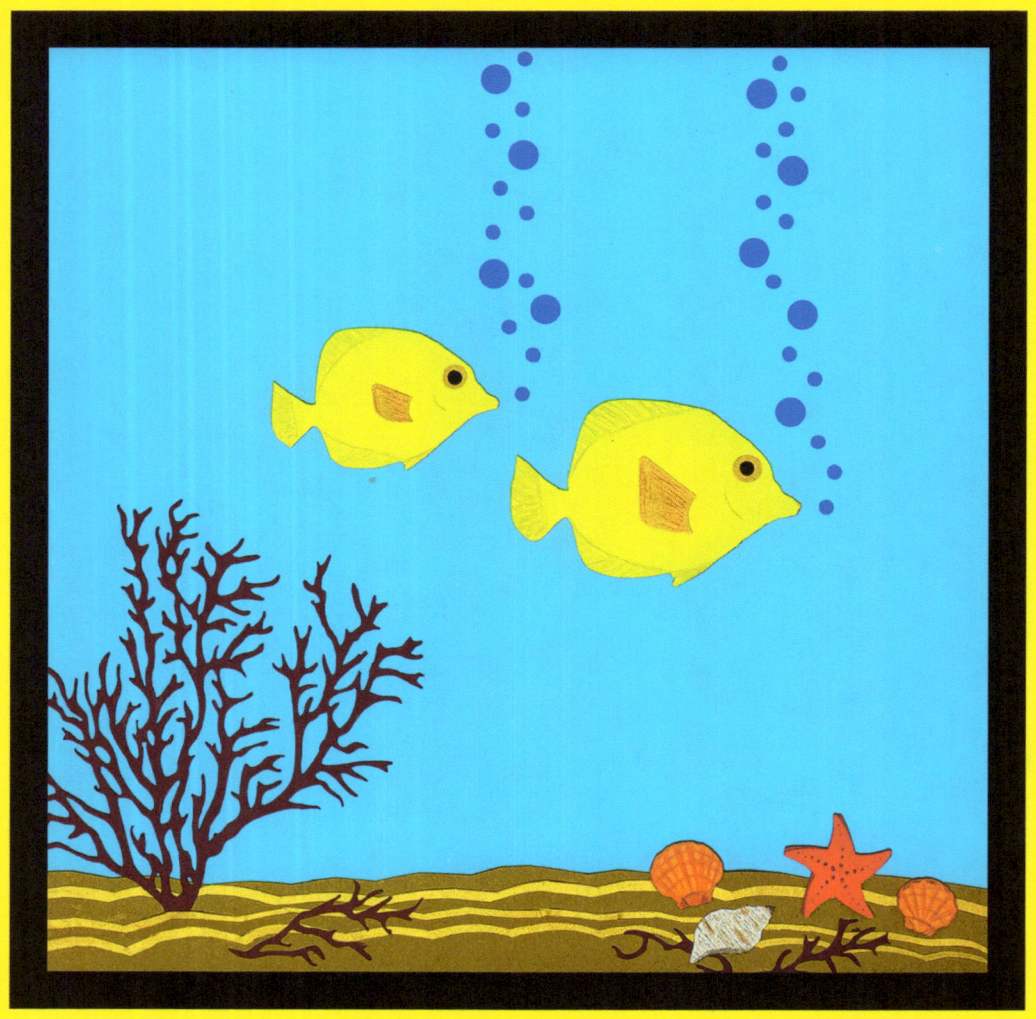

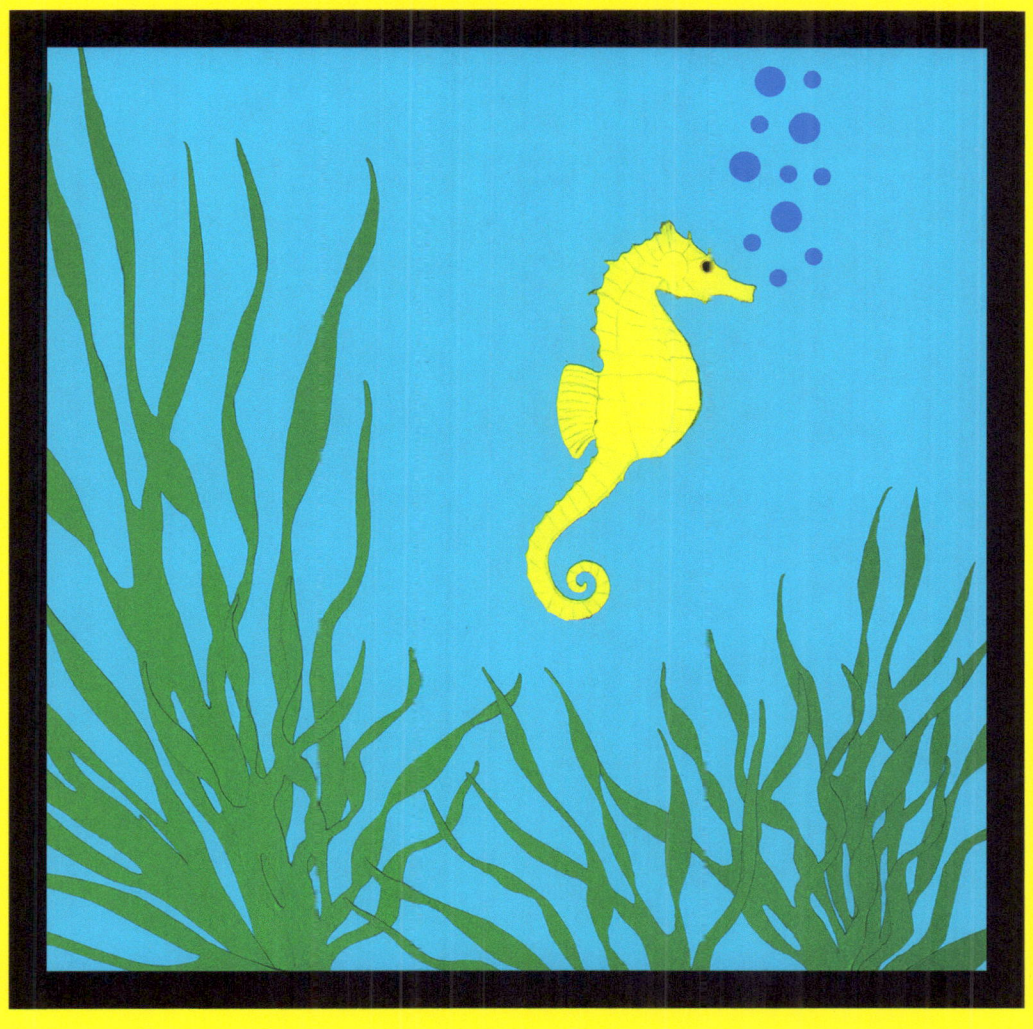

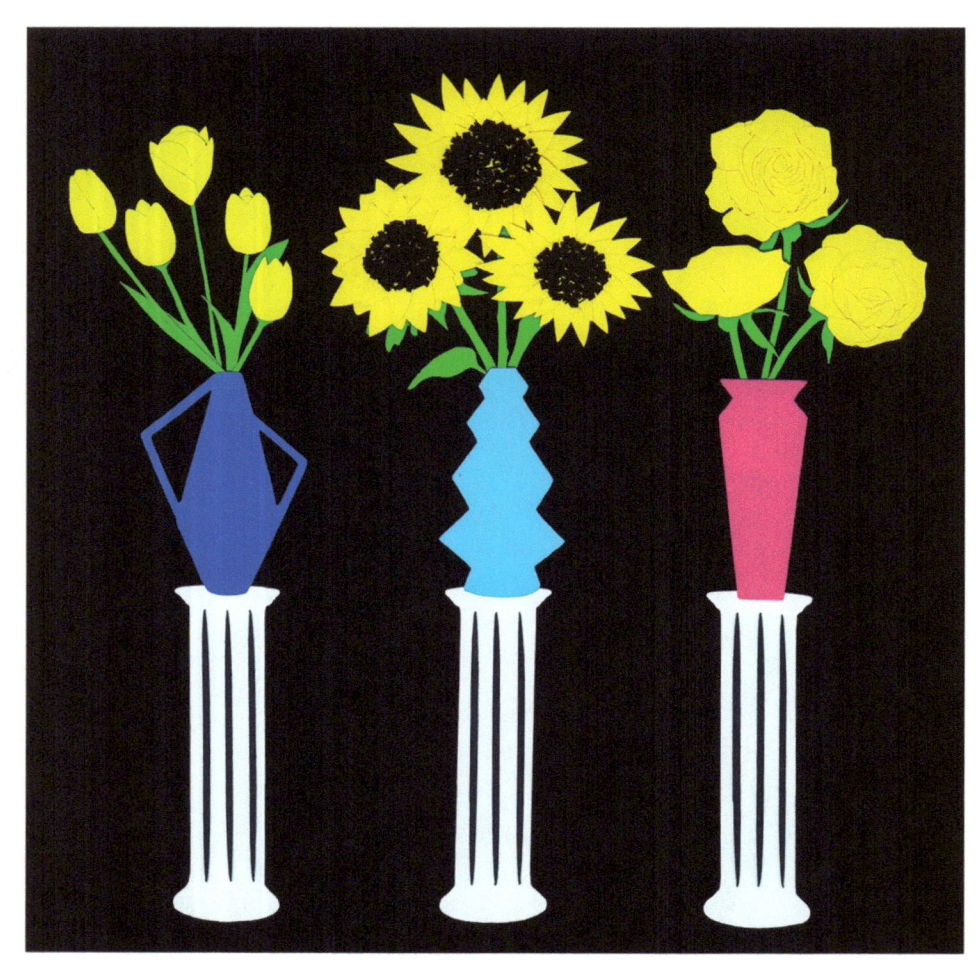

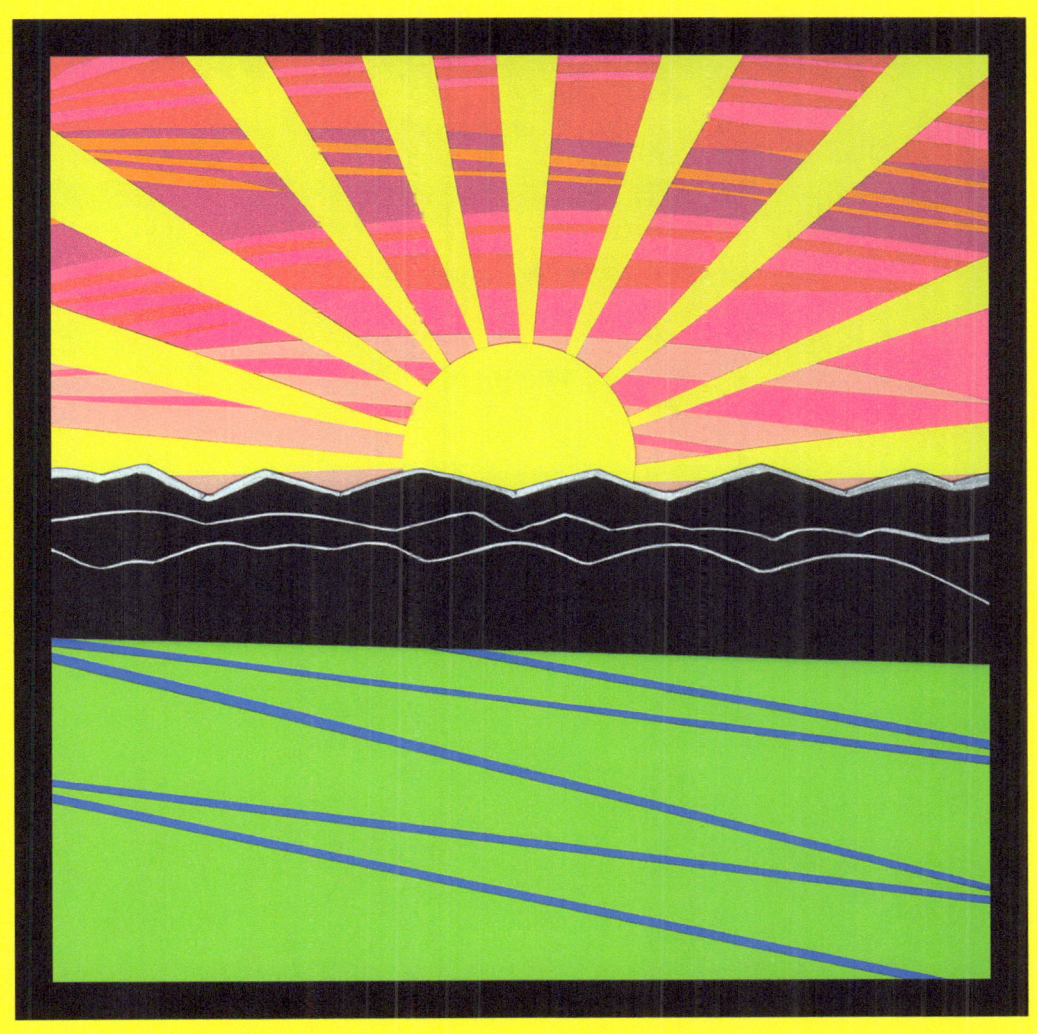

LET'S FINISH BY SAYING HELLO TO THE THINGS WE SAW THAT ARE YELLOW!

SIGN!

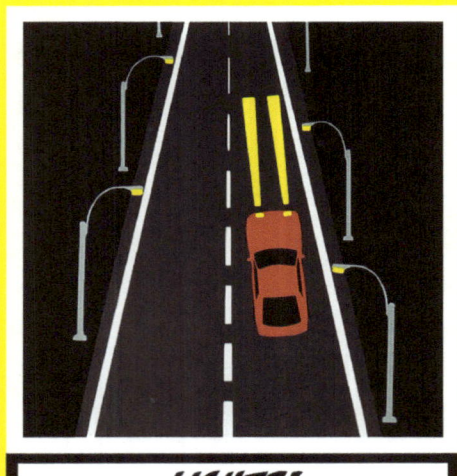

LIGHTS!

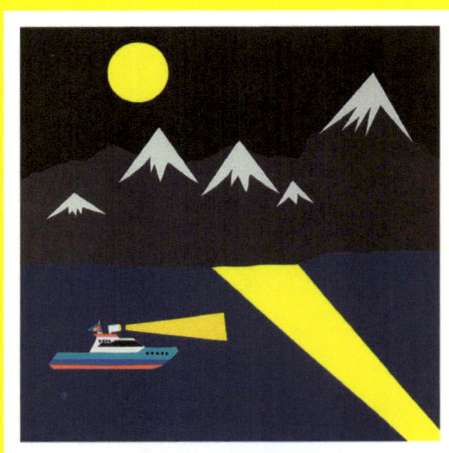

MOON!

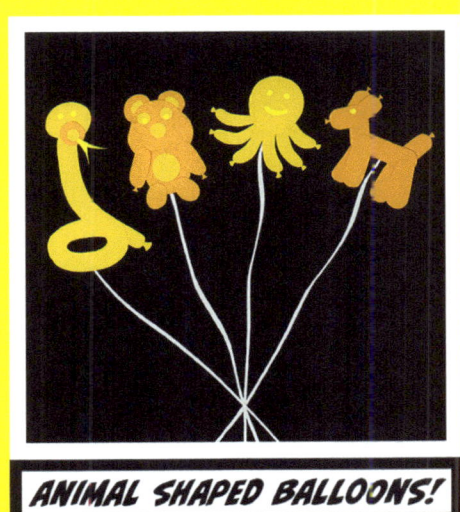
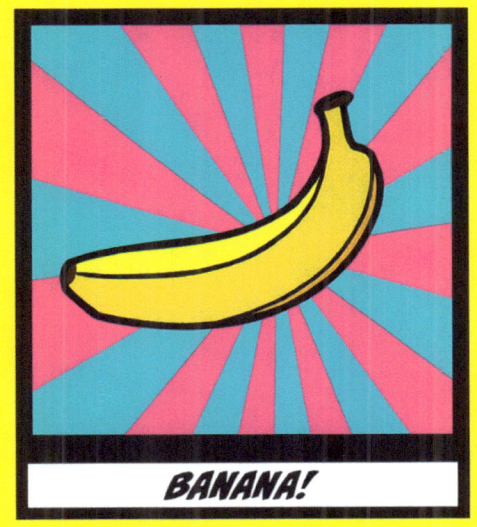
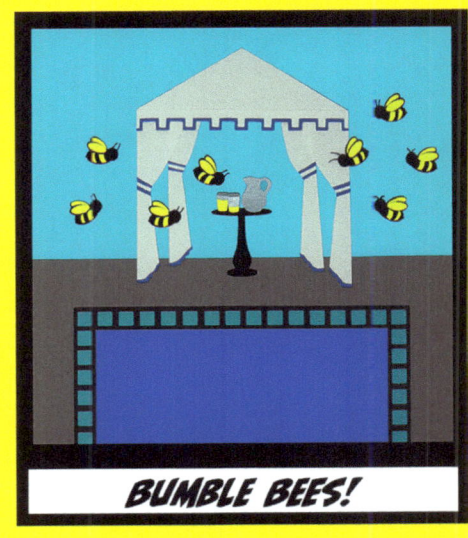
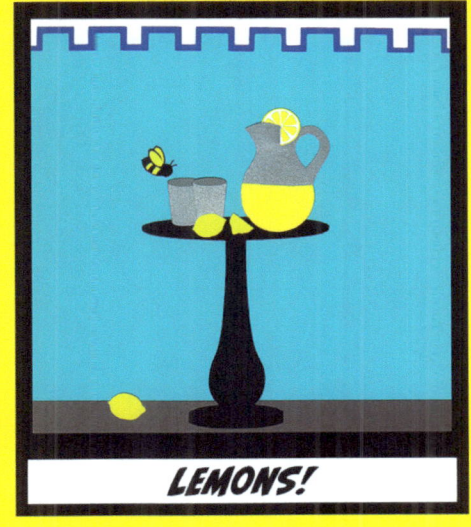

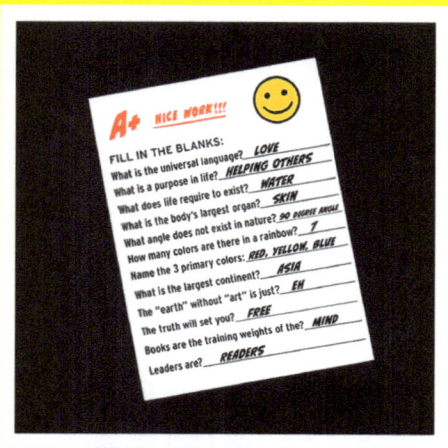

SMILEY FACE STICKER!

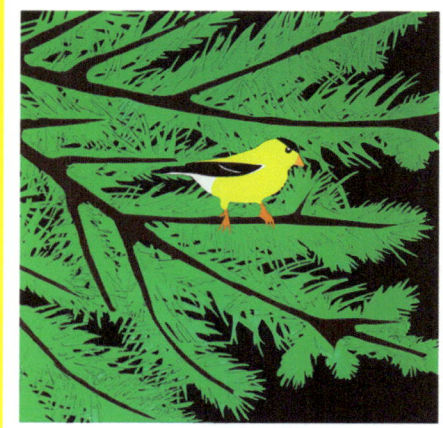

GOLDFINCH!

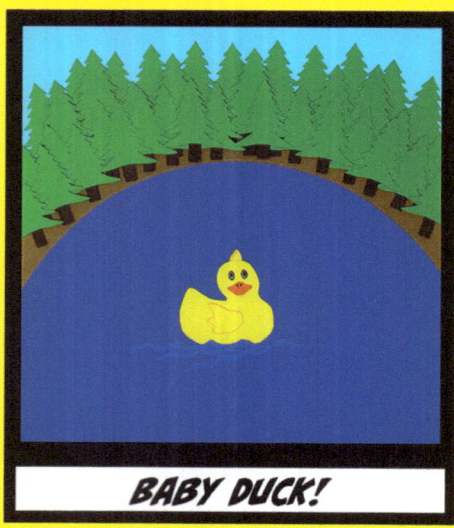

BABY DUCK!

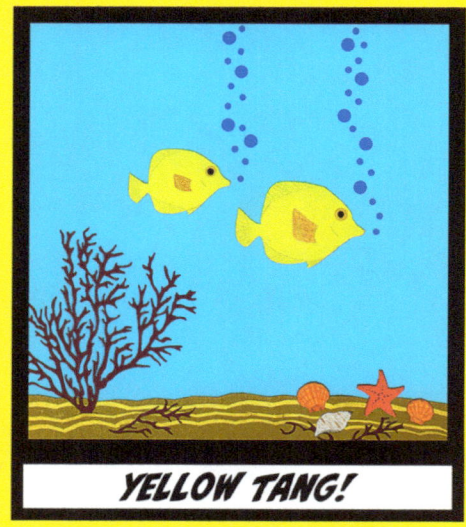

YELLOW TANG!

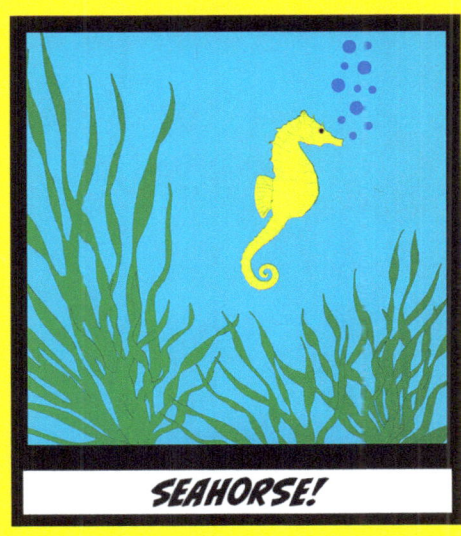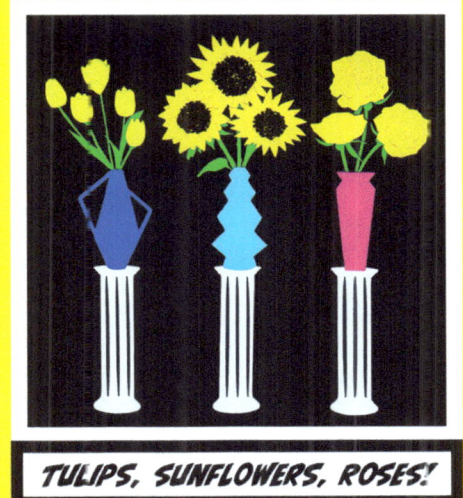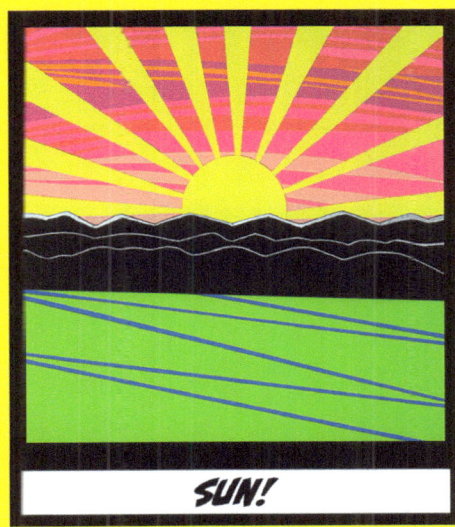

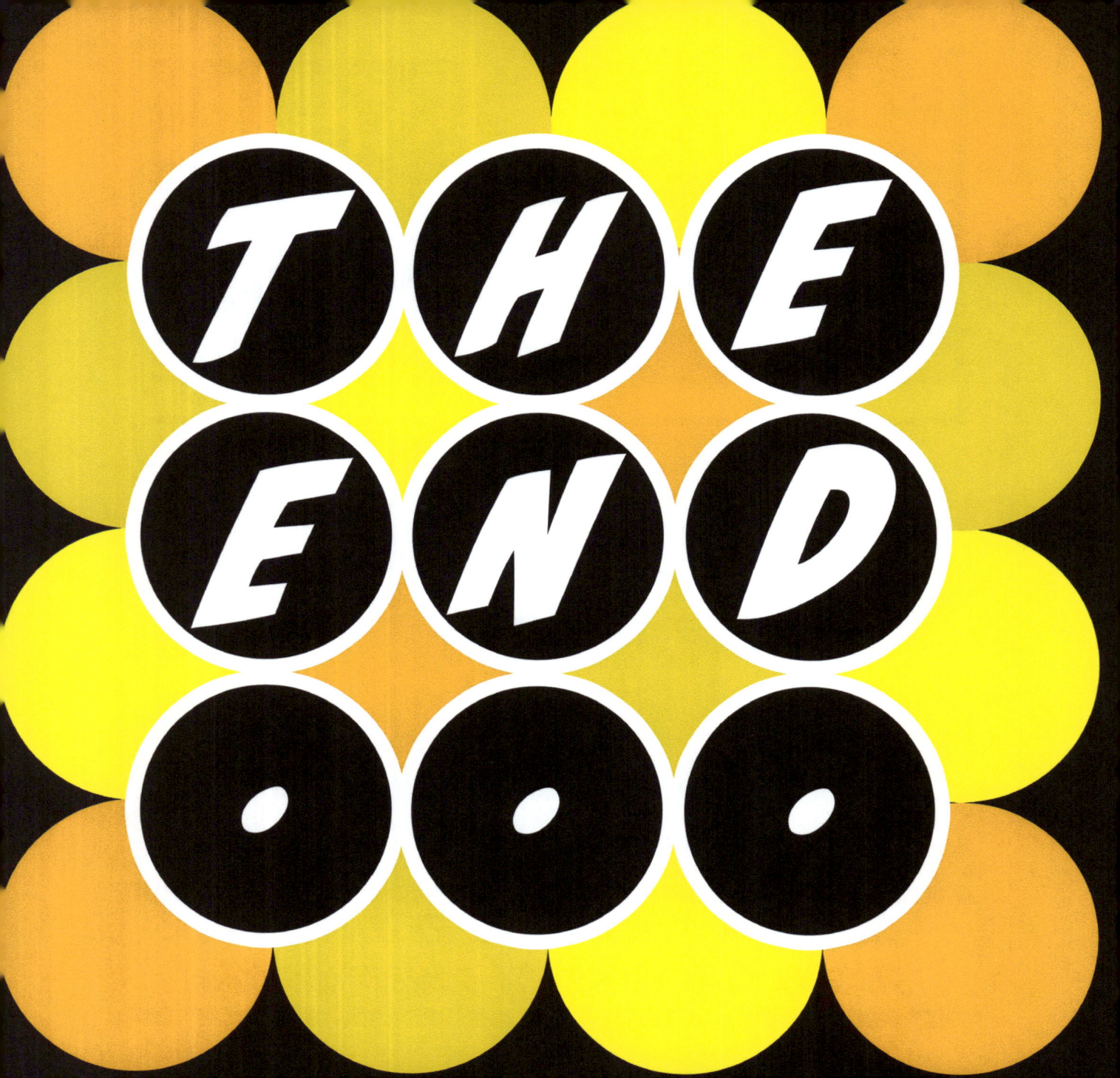

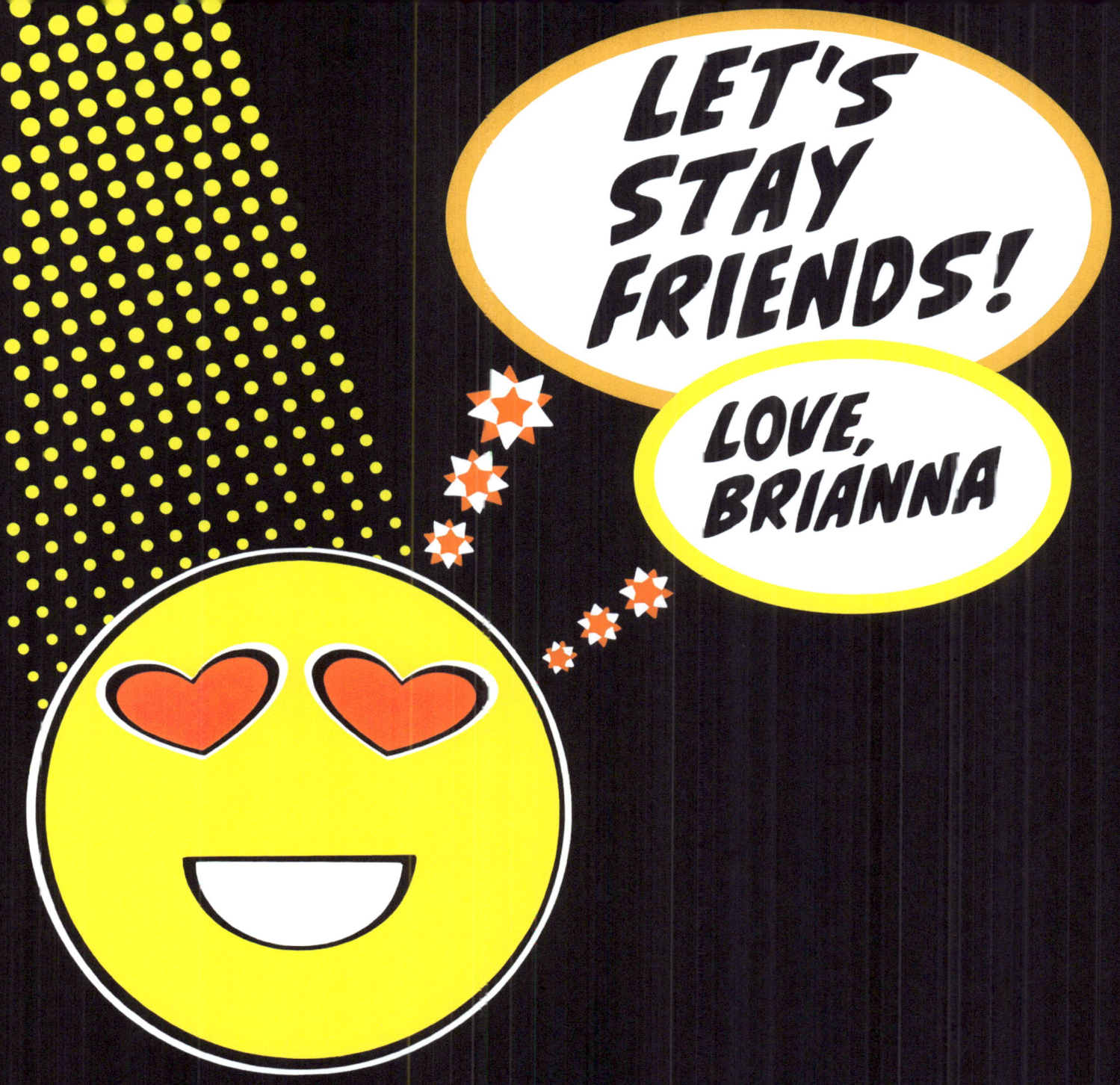

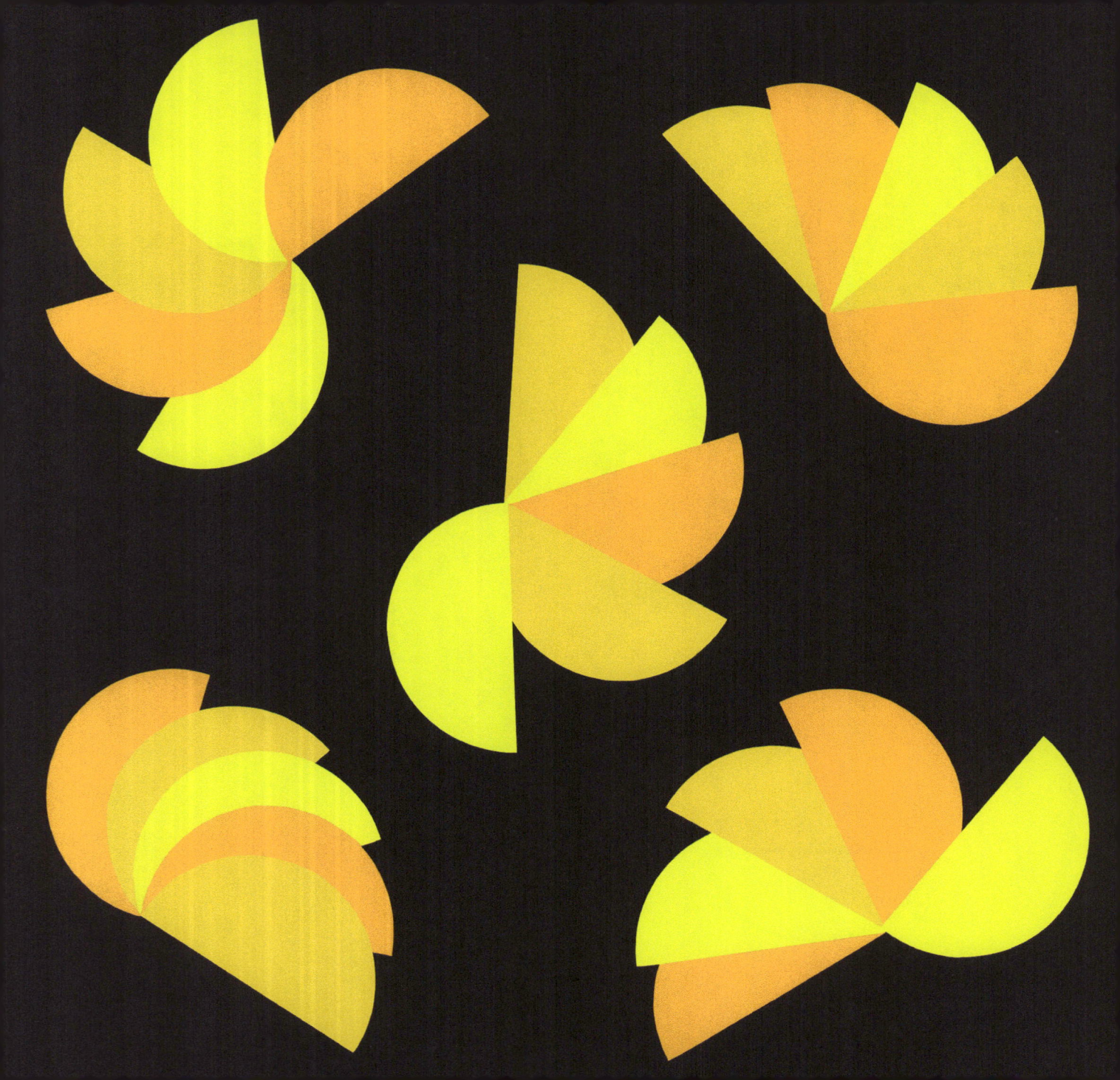

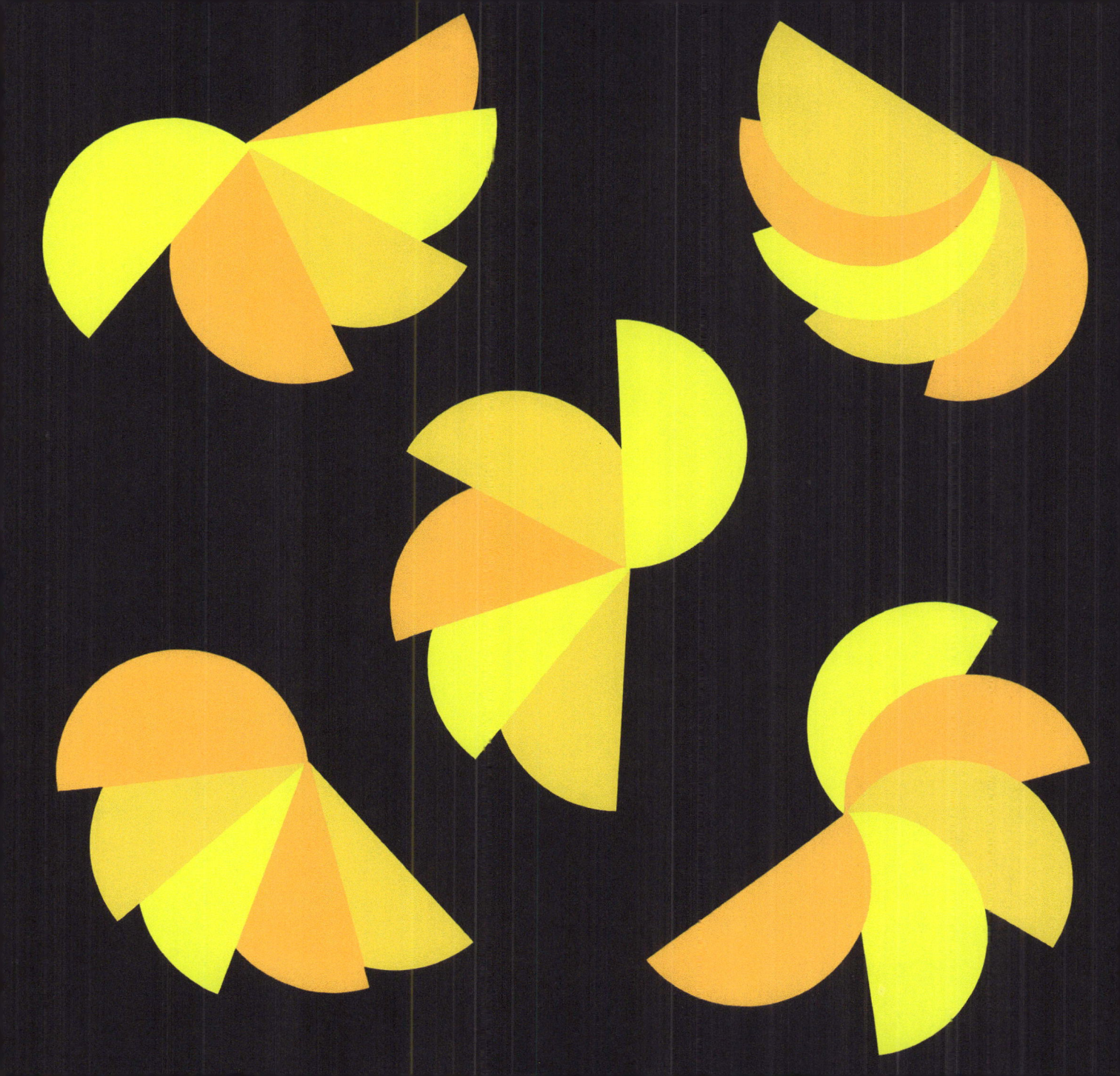

POP ART BOOKs
AVAILABLE NOW

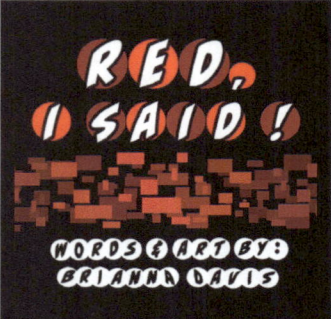
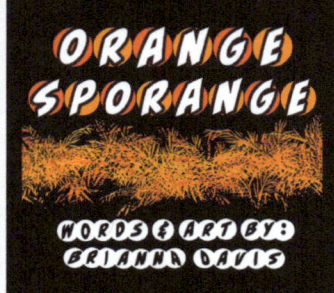
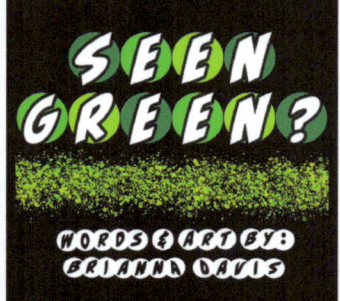
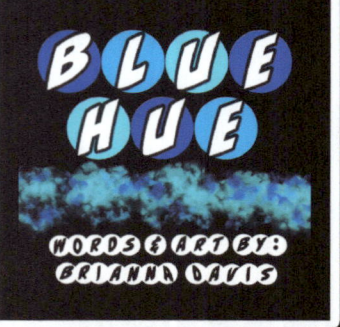
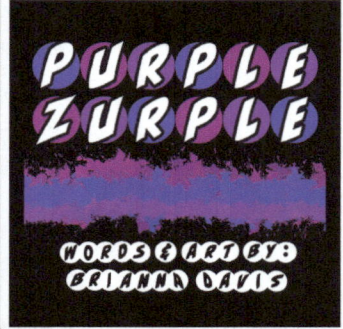
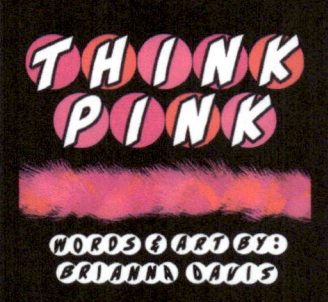
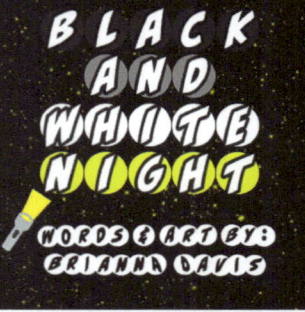
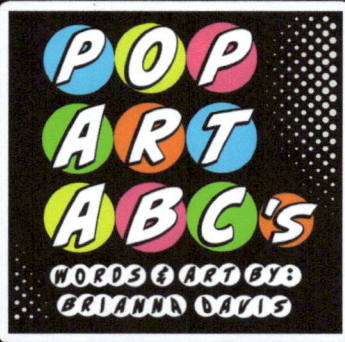
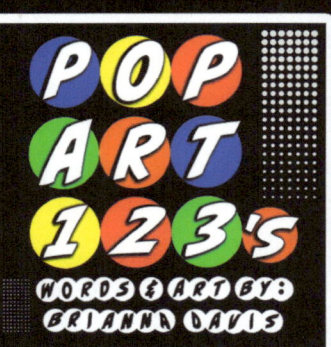